THE DIFFICULTY
OF LIVING ON
OTHER PLANETS

THE DIFFICULTY OF LIVING ON OTHER PLANETS

Poems by Dennis Lee
Illustrations by Alan Daniel

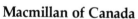

Macmillan of Canada
A Division of Canada Publishing Corporation
Toronto, Ontario, Canada

All inquiries regarding the motion picture or other
dramatic rights for this book should be addressed to the
author's representative, The Colbert Agency Inc., 303
Davenport Road, Toronto, Ontario, Canada, M5R 1K5.
Representations as to the disposition of these rights are
strictly prohibited without express written consent and
will be vigorously pursued to the full extent of the law.

Nine of these poems appeared, in earlier versions, in
Nicholas Knock and Other People (Macmillan of Canada,
1974). "When I Went Up to Rosedale" was published in
The Gods (McClelland and Stewart, 1979).

Canadian Cataloguing in Publication Data

Lee, Dennis, date.
The difficulty of living on other planets

Poems.
ISBN 0-7715-9898-X

1. Humorous poetry, Canadian (English).*
I. Daniel, Alan, 1939–   II. Title.

PS8523.E4D53 1987   C811'.54   C87-094484-3
PR9199.3.L439D53 1987

Macmillan of Canada
A Division of Canada Publishing Corporation
Toronto, Ontario, Canada

Printed in Canada

TABLE OF CONTENTS

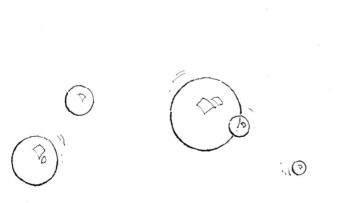

THE BUBBLE RING

When I was young,
    I did a thing
With liquid soap
    And a bubble ring:

I swished it deep
    And then I blew
And iridescent
    Bubbles grew

And drifted up
    To nudge the air,
Leaving a mental
    Shimmer there.

And though my childhood
    Days are gone,
That funny lift
    Of light goes on—

For when the world
    Is rife again
With news of war
    And acid rain,

Or when my will
    Is clenched and fraught
With worry lines
    Of *is* and *ought*,

I often sit
    And watch the way
New bubbles rise
    In the mind's display.

Sometimes they frisk
    Along in flight,
And ask no more
    Than sheer delight;

Sometimes they seem
    A concentrate
Of good and evil,
    Mean and great—

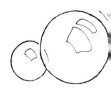

Till drifting through
    The world I see
Bright bubbles
    Of eternity.

And as they trace
    Their little course,
I feel my will
    Resume its force,

For images
    Of clean desire
Incite us like
    Refining fire,

And though the bubbles
    Disappear,
They leave a living
    Shimmer here.

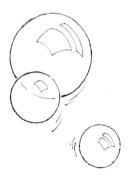

THE CAT AND THE WIZARD

I   A senior wizard
Of high degree
With a special diploma
In wizardry
Is trudging along
At the top of the street
With a scowl on his face
And a pain in his feet.

A beard, a bundle,
A right-angle stoop,
And a cutaway coat
Embroidered with soup,
A halo of smoke
And a sputtery sound—
The only real magic
Magician around.

But nobody nowadays
Welcomes a wizard:
They'll take in a spaniel,
Make room for a lizard—
But show them a conjurer
Still on the ball,
And nobody wants him
Or needs him at all.

His bundle is bulging
With rabbits and string,
And a sort of machine
That he's teaching to sing,
And a clock, and a monkey
That stands on its head,
And a mixture for turning
Pure gold into lead.

He carries a bird's nest
That came from the Ark;
He knows how to tickle
A fish in the dark;
He can count up by tens
To a million and three—
But he can't find a home
For his wizardry.

> For *nobody*, nowadays,
> Welcomes a wizard;
> They'll drool at a goldfish,
> Repaint for a lizard,
> But show them a magus
> Who knows his stuff—
> They can't slam their latches down
> Quickly enough!

II   In Casa Loma
Lives a cat
With a jet-black coat
And a tall silk hat.
And every day
At half past four
She sets the table
For twelve or more.

The spoons parade
Beside each plate;
She pours the wine,
She serves the steak,
And Shreddies, and turnips,
And beer in a dish—
Though all she can stomach
Is cold tuna fish.

But a cat is a cat
In a castle or no,
And people are people
Wherever you go.

Then she paces about
In the big dining hall,
Waiting and waiting
For someone to call
Who won't be too snooty
For dinner and chat
At the home of a highly
Hospitable cat.

And every evening
At half past eight,
She throws out the dinner
And locks the gate.
And every night,
At half past ten,
She climbs up to bed
By herself, again.

For a cat is a cat
In a castle or no,
And people are people
Wherever you go.

III   One day they meet
In a laundromat,
The lonesome wizard,
The coal-black cat.

And chatting away
In the clammy air,
They find they both like
Solitaire,

And merry-go-rounds,
And candle-light,
And spooky yarns
That turn out right.

They stroll together
Chatting still
To Casa Loma
On the hill

And there the cat
Invites her friend
To share a bite,
If he'll condescend;

And yes, the wizard
Thinks he might—
But just for a jiffy
And one quick bite.

An hour goes by
Like a silver skate.
The wizard moves
From plate to plate.

Two hours go by,
Like shooting stars.
The cat produces
Big cigars

And there in the darkening
Room they sit,
A cat and a wizard,
Candle-lit.

At last the wizard
Takes the pack
From his creaking, reeking,
Rickety back.

He sets it down
With a little shrug,
And pulls a rabbit
From under the rug.

And before you can blink
He's clapping his hands,
And there in the doorway
A peacock stands!

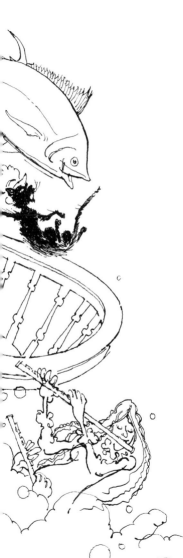

Now he's setting the monkey
Upon its head,
He's turning the silverware
Into lead,

And counting by tens
From a hundred to four
And making a waterfall
Start from the floor

And juggling a turnip,
A plate and a dish,
And turning them all
Into fresh tuna fish.

The cat is ecstatic!
She chortles, she sails
From the roof to the floor
On the banister rails,

And soon the whole castle
Is whizzing with things:
With sparklers and flautists
And butterflies' wings,

And all through the night
The party goes on—
Till it stops in a trice
At the crack of dawn,

And the wizard installs
His pack in a drawer,
While the cat tidies up
The living-room floor.

And as the sky
Is growing red,
They tiptoe up
The stairs to bed.

The wizard's snore
Is rather weird;
The cat is snuggled
In his beard—

Dreaming of tuna fish
End to end,
And rabbits, and having
A brand-new friend.

Perhaps you wonder
How I know
A cat and a wizard
Can carry on so?

Well: if some day
You chance to light
On Casa Loma
Late at night,

Go up to the window,
Peek inside,
And then you'll see
I haven't lied.

For round & round
The rabbits dance,
The moon is high
And they don't wear pants;

The tuna fish
Patrol the hall,
The butterflies swim
In the waterfall,

And high and low
With a hullaballoo
The castle whirls
Like a tipsy zoo.

And in the corner,
If you peer,
Two other figures
May appear.

One is dressed
In a tall silk hat:
The queen of the castle,
The jet black cat.

The other's a wizard
Of high degree.
The wizard is grinning.
The wizard is me.

THE BARD OF THE UNIVERSE

As I was going to the Gents
I met a man of little sense;
He was, he said, a bard in verse
Whose business was the universe.

His coat was torn, his hair was wild,
His teeth were yellow when he smiled,
And in his eyes I saw a look
So void of social sense, I shook.

"In wintertime," the person said,
"I think a little thought in bed:
'The glacial age will come again'—
And thus I see that all is vain."

I did not care for his complaint.
I urged a form of self-restraint.
But he was keen (though I was loath)
To share with me his mental growth.

"When spring arrives," the bard went on,
"I think a thought that brings me balm—
'How thrilling that the biosphere
Has joined us for another year!' "

His drift was dim, his point confused.
I did not find myself amused.
But he was keen, though I was not,
To labour it upon the spot.

"All summer long I watch the news,"
The looney brayed, "for hints and clues!
The saints and terrorists go by,
The missiles lurk—and so do I,

"Who crave to summarize in verse
The meaning of the universe,
But cannot penetrate the veil:
Does evil, or does good, prevail?"

The point was pointless after all;
I made my way to a vacant stall.
But the wretched rhymer stumbled after,
Veering from tears to manic laughter.

"Remember me," he shrieked, "in fall,
When I display no sense at all!
The birds and beetles have a home,
The fish have oceans where they roam,

"But who will say if a son of man
Can know the universal plan?"
I marched outside, in wind and rain,
And never saw his face again.

Yet ever since, when in the Gents,
I think of one of little sense:
An ancient, agèd bard in verse
Whose business was the universe,
Whose coat was torn, whose hair was wild,
Whose teeth were yellow when he smiled,
Who grieved in winter, sang in spring,
Whose tale was sheer meandering,
Who ranted on about a veil,
Who asked, Will good or ill prevail?
Who sought the universal plan,
And would not let me use the can.

THE ACADEMIC ODYSSEY OF WENDELL GREBE

When I received my doctorate, they sent me out to Calgary
And told me the experience would make a better man of me.
My name was Wendell Grebe, and my degree was semiotical,
With emphasis on Meaning, both systemic and erotical.

I taught 'From Marx to Meta-Structure' at the university
Until the students' body-language led to some adversity;
At length I pointed out, as I outdid them in mobility,
The subtext of their actions—which was reified hostility.

With that I took sabbatical from colleges conventional
And entered my vocation as a lecturer extensional.
On derricks at Leduc I urged the drillers, with felicity,
To reassess their paradigms of Trobriand ethnicity.

And when the men demurred (employing syntax loud and lyrical),
I left for Athabaska on a mission more empirical:
I longed to know if cowboys, after pedagogic seasoning,
Could learn a modest repertoire of meta-verbal reasoning.

They could indeed. And I've begun a paper deep and scholarly,
Decoding what they meant to say, when they so rudely altered me—
And proving it insane to call a neutered academic sick,
When every stinking shrink inside this unit is a lunatic!

O me, o my, o mind of mine,
I'm not the man I was:
My head is like a porcupine
Upon a plate of scuzz,
And every time I try to think
The quills begin to buzz.

I'm writing, as before, to say my talents are available
For lectureships in Meaning, with a c.v. long and mailable.
Forget my ultimatums; I will *not* object to 'charity'.
Sincerely, Wendell Grebe, in semiotic solidarity.

A parking meter told me
As on my way I went,
"You're ticking like a time bomb,
But your heart is pure cement.

"You haven't got a dollar.
You haven't got a dime.
You haven't got a lousy match
To light your coal-black mind."

He gazed upon me darkly
Till I punched him in the nose,
Then beat him with my ballpoint, till he
Tore off all his clothes.

"Hark!" he cried, "I'm actually
A Fairy in disguise!—
I tempted you with doom and gloom,
To see if you were wise.

"You pass the little Sunshine Test!
Now, here's your little Wand—"
I picked him up and pitched him
In an ornamental pond.

I don't mind parking meters
That get lippy now and then,
But I can't stand fairies coming round
And doing good to men.

A TRIP TO THE HARDWARE

I gazed around the hardware store
At nuts and bolts and nails galore,
Until the clerk, with pad and pen,
Came bustling out like a broody hen.

"Now, sir. Your lightbulb won't go on?"
"Correct. I'd like another one."
"Ah-*ha*! Perhaps we've blown a fuse?
  Or shorted out our coupling screws?

"Or else"—I sensed a faint alarm—
"Perhaps our cogs have come to harm?
  A camshaft shimmy, in a case like this,
  Is not a symptom I'd dismiss."

I blinked. "The bulb I've got is dead.
I need another bulb instead."
But this contention merely brought
A weary smile and an air of thought.

"It's not that simple, sir," he sighed,
"Your whole darn grid could soon be fried!
  We'll have to boost your juice at once
  With electro-jacks and a pair of shunts."

He dashed down figures like a man possessed:
"Take the first lot now, and we'll ship the rest,"
  Though I burst out, with a wail of fright,
  "All I ever wanted was a forty-watt light!"

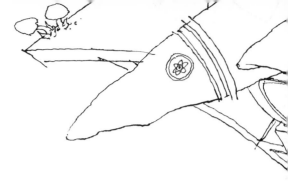

Now the man began to quiver, and he chanted in delirium
A spell to quell the gremlins and the boojums that appeared to him:
"Preserve us from the floppy faults, the downtime on the op-sys,
And the glitches if we brown-out as we access a synopsis!"

So this unexpected champion did battle with the adversary,
Routing foes who hadn't even entered my vocabulary.
"Candidly," he yodelled, "(though the thought is parenthetic), I'll
Admit the risk of techno-doom is more than theoretical—

"Because your mass is critical, we face the possibility
Of stepping up your modem to a MIRV compatibility;
A meltdown in your breeder could touch off a chain reaction
With the very real potential for a global self-subtraction!"

At this, my head and heart grew cold;
My nerves came utterly unrolled.
I took the bulb from my pocket once more,
And I set it on the counter, and I scuttled for the door.

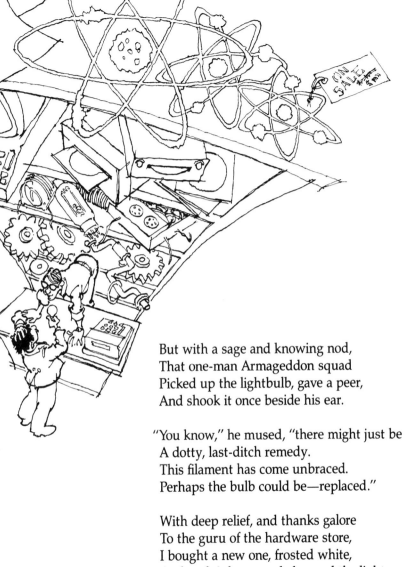

But with a sage and knowing nod,
That one-man Armageddon squad
Picked up the lightbulb, gave a peer,
And shook it once beside his ear.

"You know," he mused, "there might just be
A dotty, last-ditch remedy.
This filament has come unbraced.
Perhaps the bulb could be—replaced."

With deep relief, and thanks galore
To the guru of the hardware store,
I bought a new one, frosted white,
And took it home and changed the light.

THE SOUL OF MY WOMBAT

A Threnody

O where is the soul of my wombat,
Who used to be psychically whole?
They took him apart, to install a new heart—
But they seem to have misplaced his soul!

They checked, and they hadn't removed it,
So they searched with a CAT-scan machine;
They spotted the brains, and the heart, and the veins,
But nary a soul could be seen!

So weep for the hole in my wombat,
Which once was organically whole.
It's shiny and smart, with its spiffy new heart—
But what have they done with the soul?

THE THING

(*Robert Service meets Martin Heidegger*)

> Why do we walk every street, every block,
> And stop all the people in turn,
> Crying, "Please, if you spot the Thing Which Is Not,
> Will you beg it, for us, to return?"
>
> Take pity on three who will never be free
> Till we've paid for our childhood wrong.
> We're withered and old, but our tale must be told—
> I'll try not to make it too long.

Without a coat, without a hat,
Without a voice it came:
The Thing! the Thing! the fearsome Thing
That stopped and applauded our game.

"Ga-zookala, Matt!... Sha-kimbo, Jim!..."
We couldn't decipher a word.
But it watched us play, and it shouted, "Hooray!"
As plainly as ever you heard.

Then the three of us gawked, with a tremor of shock—
For the Thing was beginning to blur.
In a manner confusing, it seemed to be losing
Its legs, and its arms, and its fur.

And its shimmery grin, as it shucked off its limbs,
Made it pulse like a rainbow of fuzz.
The harder we stared, the less it was there;
But the instant we didn't—it was!

Why did it stay and keep bawling, "Hooray"?
Was it planning a lightning attack?
To show we weren't worried, we casually scurried
Around to our fort in the back.

Now, with no feet, no shins, no knees,
We figured the Thing would be lame;
But hoofing it hard through a dozen backyards,
Straight up to our hideout it came.

The Thing! the Thing! it started to sing,
It warbled! it babbled a joke—
And leaping and laughing and clapping its hands,
Right through the partition it broke!

I dodged to the left, Matt and Jim hung a right,
And we tore to the end of the street,
And there we looked back—with a near heart attack,
For the Thing was beginning to *eat*.

And what to our petrified eyes should appear
As the Thing went on munching apace?
It was eating its very own stomach, and wearing
A slurp of goodwill on its face—

And peeling off fingers, it gobbled them down;
And pulling off toes, with delight
It spread them unflustered with relish, and mustard,
And beckoned us back for a bite.

Then Matt was sick, and Jim was sick,
And I made a bit of a mess—
But soon we took off, for the Thing gave a cough
And it wheezed down the street after us!

So on we careened, till we reached a ravine
Where Matt thought it might have appeared,
And we made for a cave at the end of the pavement
And waited for It to draw near.

But the Thing went on shedding its body, like bedding,
By the light of the silvery moon:
One shoulder, a vest, half the ribs, and the chest—
We saw there'd be nothing left soon.

So quick as a trice, I grabbed for my knife
And I waved it three times in the air,
And cunning and brave, to the rear of the cave
I threw the knife down for a dare.

Then the Thing slithered in, with a dumb little grin,
Like fetching a stick for its friends,
And we shovelled the dirt till our fingernails hurt
And we walled up the cave from both ends.

At last! at last! the danger was past
And we threw ourselves flat on the ground,
Proud and elated, and I imitated
The way it had windmilled around.

But Jim had been thinking: the Thing just kept shrinking,
It couldn't have harmed us at all—
And maybe its scheme was to choose up a team
For hide-and-go-seek, or for ball.

And Matt started crying: the Thing was just trying
To make friends with him, Jim and me—
And sealing it in was a crime and a sin,
For it merely had wanted to be.

With sorrow that tolled like a gong in our souls,
We opened a crack in the cave;
But we'd left it too long, and the Thing was all gone—
There was nothing but dirt in the grave.

So there, in the green of the gloomy ravine,
We cried for the wrong we had done:
Whatever we'd meant, wherever we went,
The Thing was eternally gone.

And that's why we walk every street, every block,
And we stop all the people in turn,
Crying, "Please, if you spot a large Thing-Which-Is-Not,
Will you beg it, for us, to return?"

FORTY MERMAIDS

If I were swimming
In the sea
And forty mermaids
Came to me

And every mermaid
Wore a sign
Inviting me
To come and dine

With ocean heroes
Steeped in fame,
Like Captain Kidd
And What's-his-name,

And if the banquet
Hall were spread
With deep-sea ale
And ocean bread

And all the plates
Were living shells
That floated by
On tidal swells

And waiters wore
Their fin and tails
And served us each
A pinch of snails

And then dessert
Arrived in bubbles,
And everyone
Was having doubles—

I think I'd stay
An hour or two;
And then I'd swim
Back home to you.

SUZIE SAW THE BLUE BALLOON

Suzie saw the blue balloon—
And that was that was *that*;
A funny tug of otherness
Began in no time flat.

The blue balloon was soaring free
From someone's broken string,
And Suzie watched her heart go high
And felt her body sing.

It sang of ladies long ago
In tales her parents told,
It sang of setting out to sea
To find the pot of gold,

It sang a pang of leaving, and an
Ache in all things near,
It sang, goodbye to innocence
In Suzie's now and here.

And things awoke inside her
Which they'd never told her of;
But four years old is not too young
For missing what you love.

Then up the blue balloon revolved
Beyond the maple trees
Till, gaining speed, it disappeared
Like pollen on a breeze

And Suzie cried her eyes out, while
The kids and grown-ups smiled
(Except her angry parents, who had
Raised the greedy child).

When I could fly,
I'd sometimes pass
The morning couched
In meadow grass.

I'd track the ants,
Manoeuvring
To jockey home
A beetle's wing,

Or watch the way
A spider slung
Its innards out
And blithely hung—

And never spend
A thought upon
The high blue meadows
Where I'd gone.

But now the flying
Days are done,
I stake my time
To reach the sun.

The traffic and
The traffic glare
Bring back old
Arabesques of air;

That dip and swoop,
That memory trace
Still animate
This barren place

Where people scotch
Their lives for pay,
And I must serve
A desk all day—

And in my mind
I swivel high,
To claim the time
When I could fly.

BECAUSE IN ECSTASY

When I was a fresh and a freckled tyke,
My body told me what to like—
Wind on my face when the tricycle flew,
Bath and a lap when the day was through.
And what made me cry, to come in from play?
Why was tomorrow a lifetime away?
Because, because in ecstasy
I wanted it all today.

Then time began, with a hormone blur
And the prick of ideas starting to stir.
Body and mind agog with lust,
My teens lurched by as the teen years must.
Still everything beckoned and whispered, Stay!
Everything shone with its own display—
Because, because in ecstasy
I wanted it all today.

But work and the brunt of the world combined
To loosen my body from my mind.
Flesh had a thousand things to know;
Mind had matured, and told it No.
Grimly the hunches were filed away,
Dimly the body forgot to pray—
Although, although in ecstasy
I'd wanted it all today.

Now that I'm grey, I leave behind
Rule of the body, reign of the mind.
Why should I mimic my life so far?
Nothing can harness the things which are.
Winds of the spirit buffet and play,
Usher me home to the everyday—
Because, because in ecstasy
I want it all today.

THE MOUSE AND THE MAID

Epithalamion, for Susan

42   **I**   A dashing mouse, with a cool townhouse,
Was Minimus J. Magoo.
He lived by himself on the pantry shelf
At number Twenty-Two.

His parents were nice, but boring as rice.
His friends were barely awake.
Yet Minimus felt, beneath his pelt,
The soul of a rebel and rake:

For striding the streets in the snow and sleet
He never wore galoshes;
His bachelor pad was funky and bad,
With Brio and warm brioches;

And just for kicks, when up to his tricks,
He straightened his little toupee,
And he jumped in his wheels, and he kicked up his heels
And he painted the suburbs grey.

II His hero was Abe, with his sister Mabe,
And Abe was the Deli Prince,
And frequently Mini, when out on a whinny,
Would tool on down for a blintz.

And Abe and the boys would holler, "Ahoy!"
When Minimus J. rolled in,
For he was as strange, as dramatic a change
To them as they to him.

And lounging there in the musky air,
Swapping the news and sports,
He'd gaze at the knishes and bagels and kishkas,
The latkes and liver and borscht,

And he'd think, "Oh dear!" (with a muffled tear,
Which he never revealed to Abe)—
For bright as a coal, there burned in his soul
The love of a mouse for a Mabe.

III Now, Mabe had eyes like blueberry pies
And hair like a waterfall,
And Minimus J. gave his heart away,
His paws and his whiskers and all.

Yet Minimus Mouse had sought for a spouse
Since he was barely two,
And no one he'd met, not a candidate yet,
Had cherished the real Magoo;

So why should a lass with comestible class,
Exotic, yet modest and trim,
With suitors galore at the window and door
Consent to be wooed by him?

"What," he'd demand, "if she thinks I'm bland?
Or boring? or mousy? or square?"
And glumly he'd curse, crying, "Darn it!" and worse,
And slump in the musky air.

IV The suitors! the suitors! they came like commuters
In buses and pickups and carts!
For Abe was the Prince of the Kensington Blintz,
But Mabe was the queen of hearts.

The word had gone out for miles about,
The nosh at the Deli was grand—
But grander yet, in the bachelor set,
Was the hope of the sister's hand,

So through the door they streamed galore
To preen and strut their paces,
Telling her jokes, and giving her pokes,
And filling up their faces.

But Mabe, with the mien of a gypsy queen,
Served each alike in the house—
Though once in the crowd, as Minimus bowed
She murmured, "Who's the mouse?"

V First once a week, then twice a week,
Then every second day
Addressed to Abe, but meant for Mabe
A parcel found its way:

A matchbox, squeezed with ham and cheese,
Would somehow appear at the Deli;
Or a pile of Ritz and bacon bits
In cellophane, scented with jelly;

Or a lipstick, a thimble, a Valentine symbol—
And each inscribed in a blue
And meticulous hand: *"Your slave to command,
Sincerely, You-know-who."*

And grimacing, Abe, with a glance at Mabe
Would stow it behind the grill.
And silently Mabe, without looking at Abe
Would slice another dill.

VI But the suitors! the suitors! they swarmed like freebooters,
They turned her life to hell;
For Abe, though a prince, was firmly convinced
That sisters should marry well.

And daily he pressed, "Pick out the best—
Like Harvey, or Meyer, or Fred."
And Mabe would protest, "If those are the best,
I'll marry myself instead.

"They come to swill at the grill and the till,
They're hot to snaffle a wife,
But where can a wench discover a *mensch*
To cherish the rest of her life?

"Find me a man, not a flash in the pan,
With a heart like a big roomy house.
As long as the heroes are machos or zeros,
I'd rather marry a mouse!"

VII Now, today was the day that Minimus J.
Had chosen to settle his fate:
To invocate Abe, "Would you supplicate Mabe
To live as my married mate?"

But when he stepped into the restaurant's din—
The clock stood high at noon—
The very words that we recently heard
Were echoing round the room.

In the blink of an eye, the mouse chirped, "Hi!"
And tootled towards his choice—
To meet with the throb of an angry mob
And the roar of their single voice.

The suitors! the suitors! like manic computers
They spat out their envy and hate—
Till a fateful cry rose clear and high,
And Mabe came wailing:

WAIT!

VIII   *Dear Reader,*

It's time that the metre and rhyme give way to sober prose—or else the sense of mounting suspense may bring our cast to blows. (For metrical writing is known for inciting dramatis personae *to crime, while bathos and loot are the frequent pursuit of characters crazed by rhyme.)*

And yet, I confess, an additional stress persuades me to suspend it: as I contemplate the story to date, I don't know how to end it.

Does Minimus J. (as I hope) win the day? Will true love conquer all? Or is this a scene where the Guillotine of Fate must finally fall?

But with your aid, a choice can be made: in post-modernity, the reader's rights and the writer's rites can profitably agree.

VIZ:

* *If you'll kindly look at the back of the book, a ballot awaits in a slot.*
* *On the ballot, a blank: the author will thank the reader for ending the plot.*
* *To enter an Ending, just mail (without bending) your climax to this address, where plots will be counted by teams of account- ants, and literacy assessed.*
* *The unspoiled plots will be sorted in lots, perused to the final line;*
* *And the Ending voiced as the popular choice will stand as Section—*

IX(a)   The fateful cry rose clear and high,
      And echoed throughout the land:
    "A mouse may dream of a love supreme—
      And a mouse shall have my hand!"

      Across the floor, and out the door,
      And high to the sky serene
      In the whirlaway noon of their honeymoon
      A trail of gold could be seen:

      Through dawns of roving, through skies of love,
      Through memory sunsets they sped,
      And every night on a field of delight
      They spread their darkling bed.

      And the years went by in the distant sky,
      Till they shone with love as they played—
      And star-gazers christened the new apparition:
      Maximus Mouse and the Maid.

IX(b)   The fateful cry rose clear and high,
As Mabe blurted out with a wrench,
"He isn't a man—he may be a mouse—
But he, uh, seems to be a *mensch*;

"I'll have him, I guess." This qualified Yes
Brought Minimus J. to her side,
And they scuttled away on the very next day,
A blushing mouse and his bride.

But said to report, their bliss was short,
For capitalism reigned;
Ten mouths to feed, a mortgage deed,
And love went down the drain!

The house repossessed, divorce came next,
And nights in a gambling casino,
Till the mouse took a stand for the working man
And Mabe flew off to Reno.

IX(c)   The fateful cry rose clear and high:
"Remove the rodent *now!*
If it ever sneaks back, I'll hack and I'll whack
Till it looks like a plate of chow!

"Who wants to marry a critter that's hairy,
And squirmy, and bland, and smelly?"
And the suitors took scissors, and chopped off its whiskers
And frog-marched it out of the Deli. . . .

Through streets of sorrow, with no tomorrow,
Through nights where spectres thronged,
A broken mouse without a spouse
Went lonesome, lost, and wronged,

Haunting the spots where love is bought,
Its features sickly pale,
Till at the last, in a blizzard's blast
It passed beyond the veil.

X   *Dear reader, you'll see by our (a), (b), and (c),*
        The balloting led to a tie,
        And I'm quite mortified, but I still can't decide
        Which ending, if any, to try;

   And meanwhile, back at the Deli, a pack
   Of characters cool their heels,
   Asking their friends how the story ends
   And when to deliver their spiels.

   But though the plot appears to be shot,
   I'll tell you as much as I know:
   "Meyer and Harvey went off to pick larvae
   While Fred took up the banjo,

   "And Abe, who was Prince of the Kensington blintz
   (Did I mention the fact above?),
   Opened a franchise, profited branch-wise,
   And married a waitress for love,

THE END."

The Deli at last has been cleared of the cast—
Only the lovers are there,
And the fateful trill of *"Wait!"*, which still
Resounds in the musky air.

And the moment dilates, and the big clock waits,
And Mabe gives a quizzical smile,
And Minimus stands with his life in his hands
And lets it breathe a while.

There's nothing to say, and they seem to sway
Within a perpetual now,
Where borscht and a bittersweet wisdom fit
In consonance somehow.

And who can trace the difficult grace
Of a story's end? Not me.
Yet still they stand, in the near-at-hand
Of the things that are yet to be.

YER BLUES

It took a while to get to me
Because I wasn't here,
And then, despite the evidence,
The meaning wasn't clear.

The meaning hadn't felt the need
To make its presence known—
I found it down on Yonge Street, playing
Tenor saxophone.

And that is why tonight I cry
Yer lousy name in vain.
I'd do it in an artery,
Except there's talk of rain.

MR GREEN AND MS LEVINE

Mr Green and Ms Levine
Went walking by the sea.
Said Mr Green to Ms Levine,
"Will no one marry me?"

Said Ms Levine to Mr Green,
"I wouldn't care to say."
Then Mr Green and Ms Levine
Continued on their way.

THERE WAS A MAN

There was a man who never was.
This tragedy occurred because
His parents, being none too smart,
Were born two hundred years apart.

THE DIFFICULTY OF LIVING ON OTHER PLANETS

A Martian with a mangled spear
Is stuffing tarts in my left ear.
If I turn off my hearing aid,
Will I still taste the marmalade?

WHEN I WENT UP TO OTTAWA

When I went up to Ottawa,
I met a man who sang tra-la.
"What did you do with the country today?"
"I gave it away to the U.S.A."

THE PRESENCE OF PIONEERS

Out on the snow, in the deep of night,
When dogs run free and the people snore,
Beyond my window, bleached by the light,
The pioneers appear once more.

They move in groups of three, and four,
Like refugees in time of war;
Their eyes are open to the night,
Their minds reach out for something more—

As though, within a narrow room
Gone stiff and stale with old routine,
There broke in thunder and delight
One clap of what we used to mean.

Their hope sees something past my sight
As memory makes it real once more:
The curse of oceanic night,
The surge and birth of the wild green shore.

60

The Compact sat in Parliament
To legalize their fun.
And now they're hanging Sammy Lount
And Peter Matthews' son.
And if they catch Mackenzie
They will string him in the rain.
And England will erase us if
Mackenzie comes again.

The Bishop has a paper
That says he owns our land.
The Bishop has a Bible too
That says our souls are damned.
Mackenzie had a printing press.
It's soaking in the bay.
And who will spike the Bishop till
Mackenzie comes again?

The British want the country
For the Empire and the view.
The Yankees want the country for
A backyard barbecue.
The Compact want the country
For their merrie green domain.
They'll all play finders-keepers till
Mackenzie comes again.

Mackenzie was a driven man.
He wore his wig askew.
He donned three bulky overcoats
In case the bullets flew.
Mackenzie talked of fighting
While the fight went down the drain.
But who will speak for Canada?
Mackenzie, come again!

WHEN I WENT UP TO ROSEDALE

When I went up to Rosedale
I thought of kingdom come
Persistent in the city
Like a totem in a slum.

The ladies off across the lawns
Revolved like haughty birds.
They made an antique metaphor.
I didn't know the words.

Patrician diocese! the streets
Beguiled me as I went
Until the tory founders seemed
Immortal government—

For how could mediocrities
Have fashioned such repose?
And yet those men were pygmies,
As any schoolboy knows.

For Head reduced the rule of law
To frippery and push.
Tradition-conscious Pellatt built
A folly in the bush.

And Bishop Strachan gave witness,
By the death behind his eyes,
That all he knew of Eden
Was the property franchise.

And those were our conservatives!—
A claque of little men
Who took the worst from history
And made it worse again.

The dream of tory origins
Is full of lies and blanks,
Though what remains when it is gone,
To prove that we're not Yanks?

Nothing but the elegant
For Sale signs on the lawn,
And roads that wind their stately way
To dead ends, and are gone.

When I came down from Rosedale
I could not school my mind
To the manic streets before me
Nor the courtly ones behind.

THE PROTOCOL

Long ago, and long ago
And long before us all,
The daylight and the darkness
Struck a protocol.

The light would fall as boundary
On each and every thing
And coax it to coherence, in the
Shock of presencing;

But welter! welter! after dark
A metamorphosis
Would sling all things together, mixing
Glory with abyss.

So day by day the world cohered,
And night by night it flowed,
And what stood fast beneath the sun
In dark was motherlode—

For form is born in radiance,
Yet underneath the skin
The holly and the hangman share
A lethal origin.

It gives me shivers, that each thing
I love must fall away
By living its perfection, and
Survive in dark decay.

But that is how the world was tuned
By ancient protocol,
Long ago, and long ago
And long before us all.

THE REVENGE OF SANTA CLAUS

I A month before Christmas, the merchants were blue.
The people weren't buying and what could they do?
The presents were hung in the plazas with care,
And Eaton's and Simpson's had product to spare.
The snow had been spray-gunned, the Muzak was high—
But scarcely a shopper had come in to buy.

Two weeks before Xmas, the crisis was worse:
The public had fastened the strings on its purse!
Things looked so appalling, a marketing man
Worked all through the night on a devilish plan,
And corporate leaders across the whole city
Debated the scheme in a secret committee.

A week before C-Day this council of war
Which met every day on the fortieth floor,
Jamming a boardroom and baring their hearts
In a flurry of print-outs and unit-sale charts,
Reviewed all the figures, abandoned their stalling—
And cried, *"Get the santas! our profits are falling!"*
   And the marketing man took a quick Benzedrine,
   And moseyed on down to the Xerox machine.

II   In snowy cold streets, with their blanket of salt,
A holiday vision brought cars to a halt:
An army of red-suited santas, deployed
Like a shower of stars in the heavenly void,
Went creeping about in a clandestine way
Near primary schools at the noon-hour one day.

Their eyeballs, how bleary! their pockets, how bare!
But each bony hand held a treasure with care:
A stack of green flyers with lettering bold
Which they flourished like tidings of lottery gold,
Poking the sheets through the fence at each school
And whispering softly, "Pssst, kid—*Happy Yule!*"

And what was the message the schoolchildren read?
"CHRISTMAS CATASTROPHE—SANTA CLAUS DEAD!"
And proving the news to be true, there appeared
A picture of Santa Claus, *stroking his beard*,
While under the picture a large "R.I.P."
Reminded the reader of life's vanity.
    Then all over town, as the little hearts froze,
    A murmur of protest and horror arose.

III "REPORTS," read the sheet, "from the North make it clear
That CHRISTMAS will have to be CANCELLED this year:
For in a depression, the jolly old Elf
Has threatened to POISON AND STRANGLE himself!"
And then, very sadly, it told how Saint Nick
Was brooding on rumours which made his heart sick:

"Young girls nowadays are Allergic to Toys.
'Don't bug us with Presents!' implore the young boys.
The Spirit of Giving is gone and goodbye—
And that is why Santa has CHOSEN TO DIE."
("We never said that!" cried the kids in a fright,
Till the santas explained to them, "Beat it! He's right.")

And yet, in a postscript, it seemed Santa's death
Could still be averted; for with a last breath
He'd managed to stammer, "I might just appear
If kids ask for MILLIONS OF PRESENTS this year;
But otherwise—*zap!* I'm a goner for good."
     Then the children slid home in a pageant of woe,
     While the santas continued their rounds in the snow.

IV   Next morning, the city resembled a zoo,
With crowds on a rampage that eddied and grew.
(For earlier, thousands of parents had woken
To little lungs howling and little hearts broken—
Each vowing to die in the deepest of drifts,
Unless they were solaced with MILLIONS OF GIFTS.)

In a mall, a young manager gaped at the walls:
"They've cleared out a year's worth of Snugabye dolls!"
The clerks in a toyshop heard scuffles and clanks:
"They knocked Smedley out! just to get at the tanks!"
And the staff at a children's boutique gave a roar—
"Some joker just bought the entire goddam store!"

On cash and on credit! on shoestrings! on loans!
Consumers were stripping the stores to the bones!
And soon the explosion of buying had spread
To Beauty, and Bathrooms, and Car-Parts, and Bread,
Till long before evening the shops had shut tight
To load up the shelves for the morrow's delight,
    As under the moon, in its infinite sweep,
    The tide of consumers receded to sleep.

V   The week had been golden! The council of war
Reclined with a smirk on the fortieth floor
And lit up cigars, with a snifter of brandy
To toast guardian angels, if any were handy.
'Twas the night before Xmas, in fact Christmas Eve,
And takings were better than you would believe—

When out in Reception there rose such a racket,
Executives ran—and discovered *a packet!*
The thing had come crashing straight out of the blue
Through a double-glaze skylight, with nary a clue;
And once they untied it, they started to wonder
If somehow their brain-pans had broken asunder.

Inside was a letter, inviting them all
To a levee of honour at New City Hall
On the very next morning—to "thank every guest"
For "making this Yuletide the Biggest & Best."
But what prompted chuckles, and then loud guffaws,
Was the signature: *"Here's to a Killing!—S. Claus."*
   "That marketing man is a genius!" they said,
     And drank up their brandy and went home to bed.

VI At sunrise, an exquisite mantle of light
Transfigured the fall of the previous night,
As though, in the dead of the year, a new birth
Were somehow imparting its glow to the earth,
And all over town the machinery of men
Lay cradled in snow and a sleepy amen.

Yet soon by the dozen, and then by the score,
The lights of the city ignited once more.
The sidewalks were shovelled, the wreckage was towed,
As Porsches and Jaguars sprang to the road
And the warlords of Xmas, alert to the call,
Came barrelling up to the New City Hall—

And froze at the portal! For high in the sky
A tracer of light was skedaddling by;
And it hovered, then dove with a luminous whir
Till a sleigh and eight reindeer arrived in a blur,
And a fat little fellow, all crusted in snow,
Climbed out with a wink and a loud *"Oh-ho-ho!"*
    ("It's an optical trick!" said a magnate. "Big deal."
    "No way," mused another. "Those reindeer are real.")

VII   A few minutes later, a mannerly brawl
Had jammed the great foyer in New City Hall.
A throng of well-wishers applauded with pride
As the magnates were led to a room at one side,
And Santa Claus chortled, walked up to the mike,
And, tapping it once, gave his belly a hike.

"Dear humans," he started—then hooted with glee:
"There's not a soul here who believes that I'm me!
But no matter; I'm holding this special display
To honour *The Spirit of Christmas Today*.
And I trust that our guests will be welcomed like lords
When I summon them out to receive their rewards,

"For these are the folk, or the ones I could trace,
Who cooked up the scheme for our Christmas disgrace."
And the crowd with their eggnogs applauded or sniffed,
Though some were confused by the old codger's drift.
"So allow me," (here Santa Claus jingled a bell),
"To ask for assistance in wishing them well."
   With that, a trap-door opened wide as a grate—
   And up came his elves with a whacking great crate!

VIII The crowd was astonished in spite of itself—
They'd seen lots of santas, but never an elf!
And everyone smiled at the tugging and grunts
As the gruff little workers got cracking at once:
They shut the trap-door and they tidied it straight,
They pried up the lid on the whacking great crate

And half of them marched to the room at the side
Where the magnates were waiting, as if for a bride.
Then the crowd sat expectant, yet strangely serene
As they savoured the greeting-card glow of the scene—
Until at a signal the elves, in full view,
Raised a flourish of trumpets and sounded *Hallooo!*

Then Santa Claus summoned, parading in pairs,
The TOY MANUFACTURERS, clutching their wares:
Their bombers, their missiles, their cheap plastic parts,
Their guns with the power to harden young hearts.
And the elves led them out, and began the applause
As the crate opened wide—to a stupefied pause:

Then a hungry alligator crawled across the marble floor—
And it's
Crush them in! and crunch them up! or what's a Christmas for?

IX   The crowd gave a roar of spontaneous fright
As the toy manufacturers vanished from sight;
But the hubbub subsided to chirps of surprise
When the AD-MEN were called, with their slogans and lies—
And another alligator crawled across the marble floor,
And it's
Crush them in! and crunch them up! or what's a Christmas for?

Now the audience started to cheer the parade
As the BANKERS came bearing the tools of their trade:
Their loans, for the painstaking nurture of greed,
Their loan cancellations, for people in need.
And another alligator crawled across the marble floor,
And it's
Stuff them in! and munch them up! or what's a Christmas for?

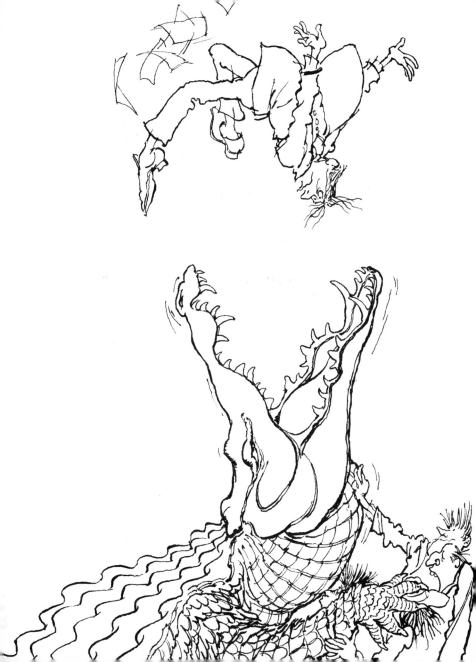

By now there was bedlam, as shoes and cravats
Of acquisitive magnates lay trampled like mats,
And Santa was forced to restrain the hurrahs
When the MEDIA BARONS came seeking applause;
Then another alligator crawled across the marble floor
And it's
Crush them in! and crunch them up! or what's a Christmas for?

The gruff little elves were all covered in sweat,
But Santa had more to congratulate yet.
There were MERCHANTS, and men of the BOOZE-VENDING CLAN,
With a place of acclaim for the MARKETING MAN—
Till at last he'd despatched the entire sorry breed
Who vandalize Christmas with cynical greed.
    Then he peered at his timepiece, observed it was late,
    And the elves led the carnivores back to the crate.

X   The crowd settled back with a gasp, as Saint Nick
Revealed how the magnates had plotted their trick:
How they'd hoodwinked the children, and blackmailed the parents,
And bastardized Christmas beyond all forbearance.
But many grew hushed as he said, deep in thought,
That morals are easy, but living is not.

"Dear humans," he mused, "you can cluck and pretend
That only a magnate deserves a bad end.
But not every rich man is greedy or cruel,
And decent folk too help to desecrate Yule;
So though it is hard, when the world's in upheaval,
To know what to worship—don't worship what's evil!"

The people stood sobered, and some could be seen
Abandoning gifts they considered obscene.
But Santa went round, speaking gently to all,
While the elves scrubbed the floor of the New City Hall.
Then on to the rooftops! and up over town!
And high to the sky as his blessings rang down:
    "Give hope to the needy; and be of good cheer;
      And here's to a warm, simple Christmas next year!"

BALLAD OF THE BONNY BIND

I had a little problem,
    Its name was Harvey Freud.
I took it to the movies, which
    It very much enjoyed.

It carried out the garbage.
    It never made a mess.
It used to come in bed at night
    And play a game of chess.

But the next-door neighbours grumbled
    With cries of very rage;
They told me, "Either neuter it
    Or keep it in a cage!"

They told me in a whisper.
    They told me in a word.
They told me through a megaphone
    In case I hadn't heard.

But a problem can't be fettered.
    Its soul is wild and free.
A problem likes to roam the streets
    At night, like you or me.

And a problem can't be neutered,
    Not unless you want a scene;
It longs for little problems
    And if not, it's rather mean.

"O who will save my problem?
　　And who will set it free?
And who will mind the bonny bind
　　That took such care of me?"

I acted in a panic,
　　I acted like a churl:
I chopped my problem into bits
　　And fed it to a squirrel.

And now I miss my problem,
　　Especially in bed.
Its name was Harvey Freud, although
　　I used to call it Fred.

THE ANT AND THE ELEPHANT

An elephant of noble stance
And philosophic countenance
Lay smitten, stricken to the core,
Beside his damaged door.

"Alack!" he sobbed, "at last I see
A home is but a mockery,
And therefore I, though big of brain,
Shall never speak again!"

Just then a brisk and friendly ant
Came by to help the elephant.
"What's up?" she asked, and turned to where
His trunk distressed the air.

"You ask me why no hope can cheer
The harmful hurt that haunts me here?—
The doors of yore prevail no more!"
The portly Plato swore.

Indeed, his door had come askew;
The lower hinge would not hang true
Because the bolt had fallen out,
Which splayed the door about.

And now the large philosopher
Unfurled a sort of verbal blur.
"My erstwhile home is occupied—
By homelessness!" he cried.

The kindly insect (who was not
Conversant with the Higher Thought)
Had meanwhile spied the bolt, which lay
A foot or two away—

And with a will she shouldered it,
Although her thorax nearly split.
"... Thus Dwelling dies, and doom descends:
Authentic Language ends!"

Then up the frame she lugged the thing
With puffs and pants and pummelling,
Until she braced it, half an inch
Above the errant hinge.

"... For what's a house without a door?
The word falls dumb for evermore;
And what is Truth, and what is Love
When Language cannot speak thereof?"

Then while he stroked his intellect,
She heaved the mighty door erect
And somehow managed to cajole
The bolt to fit the hole.

"... For Language is the deepest mode
Of all our being-in-abode;
Therefore in silence must I roam—
A mute in my own home!"

But as the metal found its place,
Her feelers caught in the narrow space;
The bolt shot home—and in she went,
A jellied accident!

This roused our hero from his pain
And, since the door was plumb again,
He stepped inside to catch his breath
And explicate her death,

And there, with pachydermic wail,
He blared the moral of our tale:
One ant, through foolish haste, may fail,
But Truth and Love will long prevail.

GREATHEART AND THE BRAIN DRAIN

Comfort me with cabbages.
My brain's not screwed in tight.
Help me plug my ears in case it
Wanders out of sight.

With a cabbage in my left ear
And a corkscrew in my right,
I forget about ontology
And I sleep just fine at night.

THE COAT

I patched my coat with sunlight.
It lasted for a day.
I patched my coat with moonlight,
But the lining came away.
I patched my coat with lightning
And it flew off in the storm.
I patched my coat with darkness:
That coat has kept me warm.

THE GOLDEN RULE

All afternoon I'd sat in school
And copied out the Golden Rule:
To keep our neighbourhood from strife,
We strive to take our neighbour's life.

"I still can't get it straight," I cried,
  As someone locked the door outside—
"We strive to take his life because
  He's taking ours, against the laws?"

"No no!" they clucked, and shone the light.
"You're only saying this for spite!
  We do it so that when he does
  We'll know he's guilty—which he was!"

"At last I see the point," I said
  As someone beat upon my head—
"To keep our neighbour pacified
  We threaten him with homicide?"

"Good boy," they smiled. "You've made a start.
  And now repeat the second part:
  Because a gun would kill him dead,
  We purchase seven guns instead."

"Of course!" I babbled into air
 As someone strapped me to a chair—
"We kill him seven times, and then
 He kills us seven times again, and
 Then we doh-si-doh some more and then the
 World—"

"No no!" they snarled, and lit the brand.
"Why can't the cretin understand?
 We flourish weapons left and right
 To show we do not mean to fight!"

I bawled, "That's what I meant to say!"
And tried to turn my head away,
And then some other things took place
Which left me with a different face,

But those are things you needn't know—
Except that when they let me go
I heard a fellow student's cries,
And turned, and met my neighbour's eyes.

TALES FROM "SIR BLUNDERBUSS"

I   Sir Blunderbuss arose at dawn
And pulled his gloves and garters on,
His suit of mail, his sword and lance,
And sallied forth in smiting stance.

Alas! what shunted into view
Was not the world Sir Blunder knew:
The streets were teeming left and right
With metal monsters, bolts of light,

And people, people everywhere
Who darted venom through a stare,
And used the manners that ensue
When chivalry is bade adieu.

"Gadzooks!" quoth he, and blinked a blink,
And sallied home again to think.

II Sir Blunderbuss in purple tights
    Resolved to set the world to rights,
    And with a fervent heart and pure
    He spurred his steed to Yonge and Bloor.

    His first opponent chanced to be
    A sorcerer, yclept "TV,"
    Who in a window by his guile
    Kept fifteen men in durance vile

    And made them praise deodorants;
    Sir Blunderbuss deployed his lance
    Like thunder on a big bass drum,
    And smote the store to kingdom come!

    Thus on a day, for all to see,
    Sir Blunderbuss subdued TV

III Sir Blunderbuss's heart was sick:
The world took chivalry for shtick!
No longer could a knight pursue
A dragon, preach, or cry *Hallooo*

Without some nosy humanoid
Unshuttering his Polaroid,
While private tourneys with his friends
Received reviews in "Lifestyle Trends."

Long, long he mulled, until the day
He saved two men from a corner fray,
And a child who saw it understood:
"That man is funny. But he's *good*."

This verdict pleased Sir Blunderbuss,
And gave him greater hope for us.

IV The metal sparked! the circuits rang!
As brave Sir Blunder faced a gang
Of rogue accountants, roaming free
With ledgers and impunity.

All week they'd terrorized the town.
All week they'd turned it upside-down
To measure glory by the ounce,
Reduce great tales to small accounts—

Till bold Sir B. had tracked the swine
(Grim pygmies of the bottom line),
And now was busy, axe and all,
Demolishing their terminal.

The caitiffs who renounced their plot
Escaped his wrath; the rest did not.

V   Sir Blunderbuss, that sturdy knight,
Espied an image of delight.
It was a maid of virtue rare,
It was a queen of soul and air,

It was a mannequin, who wore
A wedding gown in a clothing store.
An hour he dwelt on bended knee;
The damsel did not deign to see.

But on the morrow Blunder viewed
A shocking sight: the strumpet, nude
And all too plainly at her ease,
Allowed a minion liberties!

Then Blunderbuss concealed his heart,
And mocked his quest, and went apart.

VI Sir Blunderbuss could smell a doom:
He saw the mighty missile loom
And knew he trembled face to face
With the nemesis of the human race.

By now, our knight was old and worn.
Still, one last time he wound his horn
And, pledging troth to a higher power,
He hurled himself at the CN Tower!

The fight was fierce, the joust was grim,
Sir B. felt death embracing him—
Till at his final, gallant blitz
The towering missile fell to bits.

Sir Blunderbuss did not survive:
Long may his fame in story thrive.

THE DIVE OF THE TEN-TON TURD

On the day of the dive of the ten-ton turd
the banners flapped like a bird;
> the band swept by with a boom and a tootle,
> the boys came yodelling Yankee Doodle
and video cameras whirred.

The mayor, he called for his wife and his gun,
his beer and his hamburger bun,
> and he waved and surveyed the big parade,
> cheering the ten-ton cavalcade
from his platform high in the sun.

And the men gave a puff on their big cigars
and everyone planned their memoirs,
> for people all knew, and the children too,
> today was the day that our dreams came true—
the dive that would make us stars!

O, the ten-ton turd was pink and proud
as it bowed to the waiting crowd;
    then, scaling the tower, it twirled and preened,
    and out in a graceful arc it careened
and breaking the record, it—wobbled and dropped!
SPLAT! on the city it flopped & plopped,
    and bye-bye mother and apple pie
    bye-bye banners against the sky
    bye-bye drummers, bye-bye tootle
    bye-bye yodel and Yankee Doodle
    bye to the mayor, goodbye to the sun
    bye and goodbye to everyone!
(Only a glug of goodbye could be heard,
on the day of the dive of the ten-ton turd.)

THE DOUGHNUT HOLE

A doughnut hole was shining,
    Shining,
    Shining,
A doughnut hole was shining
    Above a cup of coffee.

And three white mice came riding,
    Riding,
    Riding,
Three white mice came riding
    Towards the cup of coffee.

They parked their car by the phone-booth,
    Phone-booth,
    Phone-booth,
They parked their car by the phone-booth
    Beside the cup of coffee.

They pulled out submachine guns,
  Machine guns,
  Machine guns,
They pulled out submachine guns
  Beside the cup of coffee.

They shot the hole from the doughnut,
  The doughnut,
  The doughnut,
They shot the hole from the doughnut
  All over the cup of coffee.

But the doughnut hole kept shining,
  Shining,
  Shining,
The doughnut hole kept shining
  Above the cup of coffee.

NICHOLAS KNOCK

I Nicholas Knock was a venturesome boy.
He lived at Number Eight.
He went for walks in the universe
And generally got home late.

But Nicholas Knock was always around
When the ice-cream truck went *ching*.
He dug up flowers, to watch them grow
And he mended them with string.

He found a chipmunk, shivering like a
Fur-cube in the snow.
He nursed it through to the end of March
And then he let it go.

Acres of grass and acres of air—
Acres of acres everywhere:
The sun shone high, and the moon shone low
And Nicholas didn't care.

So Nicholas Knock went doodling
Through summer & winter & spring.
His mind had funny edges
And the ice-cream truck went *ching*.

II One year it was Tuesday; Nicholas Knock
    Went noodling off for a bit of a walk.
    He hid on his brother; he raced a dog;
    He helped a little kid catch a frog.
    Then at the curb, and walking east,
    He spied the silver honkabeest.

    A trick, a flicker of the light:
    The tiny creature, like a flight
    Of warblers, seemed to ride the air
    And shed a frisky lustre there.
    And yet it did not move a hair.

    Its eyes were dusky, deep, and clear.
    It rose; it flew; it settled near
    And Nicholas stood by its delicate side,
    Nicholas stood and almost cried.

    He left it then, but all that night
    He dreamed of its radiant arc in flight.
    And when he returned in the morning, the air
    Was dimpled with light and the creature was there!
    And every day, for a month at least,
    He met the silver honkabeest.

III   "O mother, dear mother
      Prepare us a feast;
   I'm friends with the silver
      Honkabeest!

"Oh father come quickly,
    I want you to see
For it's shiny and gentle as
    Gentle can be."

"Nicholas Knock!"
   His parents hissed,
"That honkabeast
   Does not exist!"

But Nicholas whinnied,
   And Nicholas sang,
And Nicholas hopped
   Till his bell-bottoms rang.

"I've seen it! I've seen it!
   I'm practically sure!
We meet every morning
   At Brunswick and Bloor."

His parents sat down,
   Exchanging a glance—
Alas for their son
   With his weirdo dance!

Even the neighbours
     Were starting to talk:
What was the matter
     With Nicholas Knock?

His mother declared,
     "I wish I was dead!"
And all in a fury
     His father said,

"This neighbourhood
     Should be policed
To get that vicious
     Honkabeast!"

But Nicholas figured,
     Their tempers would mend,
So Nicholas tore off
     To visit his friend.

IV "Frisky, most silver, serene—
     bright step at the margins of air, you
tiny colossus and
winsome and
master me, easy in sunlight, you
gracious one come to me, live in
my life."

They took him to
     A specialist
Who soon prescribed
     An oculist
And then a child
     Psychologist
And last a demon-
     Ologist,
Who knew about
     Astrology
And dabbled in
     Phrenology.

Their diagnoses
     Disagreed,
But on one thing
     They all agreed:
If Nicholas Knock's
     Delusion ceased
(He thought he saw
     A honkabeast),
The boy would mend
     Within a year;
But otherwise
     His fate was clear—

A life in hospitals,
  Designed
To pacify
  The deviant mind,
A life in
  Institutions, meant
To exorcize
  Such devilment;
But still the boy
  Could be released
If he gave up
  His "honkabeast."

Yet heartless, witless,
  Stubborn and slow,
Nicholas Knock
  Kept murmuring, "No."
They yelled at him,
  They shed real tears
Till Nicholas finally
  Plugged his ears;
The more they told him
  "Kill it dead!"
The harder Nicholas
  Shook his head.

At last they cried,
    "His time is short:
Take him away, to
       Supreme Court!"

VI   *Snort!* went the
    Court clerk, and
    Pounded on the table-top.
   "Stand!" cried the
    Bailiff with a steely-eyed stare.
   "Name?" shrilled the
    Registrar, and
    Poked him with a fountain-pen.
   "Swear!" boomed the
    Justice with a glare.

   "P-p-please," stammered
    Nicholas, "I've seen the silver
    Honkabeest—"
   "Silence!" roared His
    Lordship, "that's a rumour and a lie!
    Poppycock and insolence! The
    Honkabeast is *not* a beast—
    How are we to know it's not a
    Pervert, or a spy?
    Eh?
    It's probably a pervert *and* a spy.

104   "Unless you sign a declaration
        That the Honkabeast is fiction,
        Then I must—as a precaution,
        To preserve Confederation—
        Place a legal limitation
        On your circumambulation
        With a minor operation
        Which we call decapitation."

            Nicholas stood,
            He quivered with fear
            As he uttered the words
            Which I set down here:

        "I'm frightened of burglars,
        I shake in the dark,
        And I'm scared of your sharp sharp knife;
        But I love the silver
        Honkabeest
        More than I love my life.

        "I will not sign your paper.
        I will not sign your bill.
        I've seen him every day for a month
        And I hope I always will."

VII   The registrar spoke

    With a dry little cough.
"The lad," she observed,
    "Simply won't be put off;
Perhaps we should listen,
    And not merely scoff?"

But His Lordship was raging,
    He pounded and said,
"Take out the rascal and
    Chop off his head!—
And by midnight tonight
    There'll be two of them dead!

"For the army, the navy,
    The Mounted Police,
The bailiff, the sheriff,
    And I
Will personally go
    To the Honkabeast's den,
Preparing to do
    Or to die.

"With thousands of soldiers,
    And bombs in each hand,
With missiles and
    Submarines—
To safeguard our children
    We'll blast it and blitz it
To billions of
    Smithereens!

"And at last this land
    Will be released
From the threat of the terrible
    Honkabeast!"

VIII   Now Nicholas Knock was a logical boy,
        His powers of thought were good,
    But sad to relate, a legal debate
        Was more than he understood.

    His head was all cluttered with *right* and *wrong*,
        And *things you mustn't do;*
    His mind was all muddled with *evil* and *good*,
        And *"Lies are never true."*

    So he stood like a stick, and his eyes looked sick,
        Till he uttered a piercing cry:
    "The honkabeest isn't fiction—
        And the honkabeest won't die!"

Thump! went his
Fist upon the
Forehead of the clerk of court—
Crack! went his shoes against the
Sheriff's bony shin—
Squelch! as his head hit
The bailiff's bulgy stomach, and—
Crrunch! as he caved His Lordship's
Hearing-aid in.

> Then Nicholas whizzed
> And Nicholas whanged
> And Nicholas knocked
> Till their craniums rang.

He covered them in legal briefs,
   He threw them on the floor,
He rolled them up in carpet from
   The courthouse corridor.
He hung them from the curtain rods,
   He coated them in foam,
And told them, gently, "Leave the silver
   Honkabeest alone."
And then he pulled the ceiling down
   And made his way back home.

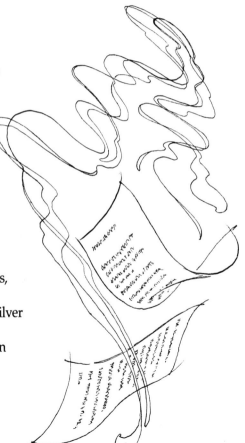

IX The sky was as blue as a clear blue sky,
The sun was hot and high,
When Nicholas came with a flick in his step
And a fidgety glint in his eye.

The city hung around him, like a
Quick and dirty scrawl:
The traffic lights, the neon lights,
And the Bank of Montreal.

He never looked to left or right;
He came home straightaway
To where the silver honkabeest
Had met him every day.

He watched the stores; he watched the cars;
He spied a silver light
That winked at him, and blinked at him—
And disappeared from sight!

And hunting round to find the thing
He thought he heard a hoof
That clickered like a honkabeest's,
But vanished without proof.

And here a snort, and there a tail,
    And silver without end:
He spent a day and night that way,
    But he couldn't find his friend.

But neither could he give it up
    (And this is what was queer),
For every time he started to,
    The thing would reappear

And light would flicker, light would fizz
    Like whispers made of steel,
Till, silver in its secret life,
    The city felt like real.

And if you take a walk on Bloor
    You still can see a boy
Whose face is sometimes in despair
    And sometimes full of joy.

You'll see him stalk and whirl around
    A hundred times at least.
Don't bother him! He's hunting for
    A silver honkabeest.

X Frisky, most silver, serene—
   bright step at the margins of air, you
   tiny colossus and
   winsome and
   master me, easy in sunlight, you
   gracious one come to me, live in
   my life.

ODYSSEUS AND TUMBLEWEED

Odysseus and tumbleweed
And Paddle-to-the-Sea—
All the famous wanderers,
Calling out to me.

Come away, and come away,
And come away with us,
Harbingers and heroes, on
The journey perilous.

Here I sit and sign my name
To endless paper chains—
Odysseus and tumbleweed
Still chafe within my veins.

Come away, and come away,
And come away at last;
How should you be shacking up
With comfort and the past?

Canada is burning, and I
Could not tell you how—
But Paddle-to-the-Sea is sailing
Wide, and leaving now.

Come away, and come away,
And come away alone;
Follow to the living source
Before you turn to stone.

Here-and-now is real, and I am
Pregnant with the yen,
Yet heroes of the distance draw me
Out beyond my ken:

Odysseus and tumbleweed
And Paddle-to-the-Sea—
All the famous wanderers,
Calling out to me.